Inspiring Shes

Power. Inside and Out.

The Power of Self - Tricia Mahoney

The Power of Intent - Nora Cabrera

The Power of Spaces - Wendy Sippel

The Power of The Body - Dr. Jennifer Beights

The Power of Image - Lisa Avila

The Power of Patterns - Brizel Granados

The Power of Balance - Stacey Stier

Cataloging-in-Publication Data available from the Library of Congress.

ISBN-13: 9780615915999
ISBN-10: 061591599X

For every SHE.

I AM SHE.
POWERFUL. VISIONARY. HONEST.
TRUE. TRUTHFUL. GRATEFUL.
STRONG. **LOVING.**
PASSIONATE. KIND. BRILLIANT.
COURAGEOUS. UNDERSTANDING.
EMPOWERING.
FREE.
DRIVEN. BRAVE. CURIOUS.
CREATIVE. CONNECTED.
DEEP **ACCEPTING.**
DETERMINED. CALM. GENTLE.
COMPASSIONATE.
GOOD.
RELIABLE. POLITE. DILIGENT. FUNNY. GENTLE.
HELPFUL. **FEARLESS.**
PATIENT. NICE. DYNAMIC. TRUE.
HARD-WORKING.
OPTIMISTIC. MODEST. INDEPENDENT.
IMAGINATIVE. KIND.
POWERFUL.

I AM
CONFIDENT
POSITIVE
COURAGEOUS
VALUABLE
WORTHWHILE
LOVE ME FOR ME
TO INSPIRE HEALING
STRENGTH
ASPIRE
TRUST YOUR INNER SELF
LOVE YOURSELF
BELIEVE
IN YOUR
FUTURE
YOU ARE
WORTH IT

I CAN
DO ANYTHING
BE THE BEST ME
TRUST
BELIEVE
EXPECT SUCCESS
PURPOSE
POWER
DREAM
ACHIEVE
TRUST YOURSELF
YOU ARE THE
PERFECT YOU
FOLLOW YOUR DREAMS
THEY KNOW THE WAY
JUST BE

YOU ARE EXACTLY
WHERE YOU ARE
SUPPOSED TO BE
SPEAK KIND
WORDS AND
THINK KIND
THOUGHTS
TO INSPIRE
LOVE STRENGTH COURAGE
GRATITUDE FORGIVENESS
TRUST TRUTH
LOVE
STRENGTH COURAGE
GRATITUDE FORGIVENESS
TRUST AND TRUTH
SHE TO SHE

Preface

Inspiring Shes is a collaborative collection of seven chapters written by seven different women with the common goal of motivating and empowering other women to attain their truest and best version of themselves. Separately, each chapter was written from the perspective of the author based upon her experiences, both personal and professional. Collectively, the chapters are representative of a wide range of topics presented to inform and inspire.

Just as your path is different from ours, the views expressed by each co-author are individualized. Our goal is that you will take from this book what you need to find and grow the Power within you.

Contents

Chapter 1: The Power of Self   3
by Tricia Mahoney

Chapter 2: The Power of Intent   21
by Nora Cabrera

Chapter 3: The Power of Spaces   37
by Wendy Sippel

Chapter 4: The Power of The Body   53
by Dr. Jennifer Beights

Chapter 5: The Power of Image   73
by Lisa Avila

Chapter 6: The Power of Patterns   85
by Brizel Granados

Chapter 7: The Power of Balance   99
by Stacey Stier

Inspiring

Shes

One

The Power of Self

by Tricia Mahoney

Self is inward. It is private. Self is your deepest dreams and greatest aspirations. It is your assets, vulnerabilities, body, mind and spirit. It's your truth; what you want, who you are and who you want to be.

I don't think I ever thought about *self* as its own entity. I've thought about self-confidence, the times in my life when I've had it and times when I've needed it. I've thought about words like selfish and selfless, but never about *self* as separate. Then I began my journey of self-discovery.

A few years ago, as my marriage came to an end and I was going through a difficult divorce, I was forced to evaluate where I was and how I got there. I realized that during the many years I was married, I cared for and catered to everyone in my life while stifling my own needs, wants and desires. While I was living my perfect, pretty, married life I abandoned me. The real me.

This realization was devastating. I didn't know who I was, what I wanted or even who I wanted to be. Looking back I see that losing myself in that way prompted the change that was absolutely necessary to getting back to my true self. But back then I just felt alone, wounded and raw.

While trying to survive the changes in my life I went through different stages of healing. This journey of self discovery has been the hardest thing I have ever gone through, but what I found along the way were seven intents that seemed to continually resurface; *Love, Strength, Courage, Gratitude, Forgiveness, Trust, and Truth.*

Each of these intents really resonated with me. I tried to live by them everyday - sometimes

I would temporarily master one intent and move on to another and other times I felt stuck, unsure of how to move forward. But I yearned for change and growth and was fully committed to this process. I believed it was my path, and to move forward I had to uncover my truths to rediscover myself.

It was many months before I even began to recognize myself and what I wanted in my life but through it all these seven intents became my rules. The laws I learned to live by.

Love

I didn't recognize this strange, co-dependent woman I had become. I wasn't strong. I wasn't true. I didn't listen to what I wanted or needed. I was selfless to the point of destruction and I was voiceless. I ignored my needs while catering to everyone else's. I thought I was being the best wife, mom, daughter, sister, daughter-in-law and sister-in-law by focusing my love and attention outward. I focused so much on everyone else that I got lost along the way.

I was under the impression (delusion) that love was only two things: my love for others and their love for me. I didn't understand that *love of self* is the root of all love. My issue with love was that I simply didn't love myself.

This realization both derailed me and transformed me. I needed to take responsibility for where I was and the path that I was on. I needed to accept me and love me for me; my greatest assets and my beautiful flaws. I needed to love me. Acknowledge that I am human. Lovable. Loved. Special. Unique. That my assets and my flaws are what make me - ME. This was the beginning of my discovery of *self.*

I started to listen to my heart. I cleaned house by releasing unhealthy relationships, which was an enormous challenge for me because I am non-confrontational. I want everyone to like me and I want everyone to be happy. But realizing that I was not being treated well by some of the people closest to me was sobering. These people needed me to be weak and indecisive, but I wasn't that person anymore. I started to stand up for myself and stand my ground. I distanced myself from anyone who didn't want me at my best and what was best for me. Consciously changing these relationships was the first step. If I wanted to be the best me, I needed to be surrounded by people who wanted the same for me.

Taking responsibility for my relationships was empowering.

Next, I quieted the internal chatter filled with fear, worry and darkness. Muting these toxic thoughts was difficult but replacing them with hopeful positive thoughts seemed to work. The more I focused on hope, peace and happiness the calmer I felt. The toxic chatter quieted and my deepest desires and truths began to emerge. I started to see my path, my purpose, my intent. The direction I wanted to head in became very clear to me.

Listening to myself felt good. I began to gain strength.

Much of what had been important to me became less important. Almost insignificant.

The simple things - spending time loving my children, eating meals together, talking about our day, our successes, our failures, our lives - became my focus. Enjoying time with friends. Living each moment, all in. Work when I work, rest when I rest and play when I play. By keeping these things separate I find that I am better able to focus on the who and what of the moment.

Slowly my love of self began to take root. I started to focus on loving and trusting myself. Listening became easier and my intent become clearer and clearer. What I wanted, from the deepest part of me, started to unfold. I became more confident. I felt good in my skin. The real me was coming back.

I began to develop strength and courage...

Strength & Courage
Strength and courage go together because when you have strength you gain courage and when you are courageous you become stronger.

I am a person with inner strength. When I know what I want I go out and I get it. But when I was weak, so was my strength and courage. As my inner truth was revealed I gained courage, and with every ounce of courage I gained a little bit of strength. Some days tested my courage and strength and some days depleted it, but by continually connecting back to my inner voice I was able to keep moving forward on my path.

On my darkest days I would recite this personal mantra:

I am strong. I will find peace. I will be true.

Saying this out loud grounded me, calmed me and kept me moving forward.

Being strong and courageous is also strategic. There were people in my life that made me feel weak and meek. But that was my issue because I allowed myself to be weak and meek. I knew I needed to find my voice, to literally speak up for myself and voice my opinion. Be heard. For me, it was about saying less and holding strong.

I hated the fact that I allowed myself to be powered over so I came up with a few statements that worked very well for me. "I'd rather not," and "I wished I could, " became my answers. So simple yet so powerful!

Whenever I felt pressured or bullied I would simply respond with one of these statements then wouldn't say another word. The silence was uncomfortable but it worked! There is little somebody can say after hearing a statement like that. They are polite words, yet very strong words, and they allowed me to stand my ground and do what was right for me. This was a breakthrough for me. It was strength in voice and opinion and it was exactly what I needed.

I discovered that courage is learning how to stand up for yourself, your wants, your needs and your desires. And strength is the fuel for courage. Be strong and find the courage to protect and portray the most perfect expression you.

Gratitude & Forgiveness

I always thought that I was a thankful person but going through this process of self-discovery made me realize that, although I said thank you all the time, I was not truly thankful for what I had in my life. I contributed to the society of more, more, more. The latest, the greatest, the upgraded. My blind and misguided behavior was shopping for clothes, shoes, handbags and accessories. As an Image Consultant I shopped for a living so it was the perfect job for me. What I didn't see was that I was filling my closets with expensive things that I didn't need. Things that didn't bring me joy. I was filling my closet instead of filling my heart and I was never satisfied because it wasn't what I needed.

Now I see with different eyes. I don't want for excesses anymore because I see what I have in my life: my children, my family, my friends, my home and my life. I am happy and so very thankful for all that I have.

During my divorce I felt devastated. I was angry, mean and sometimes rude, but the bottom line was that I couldn't cut my ex out of my life because we have children together. I began to see that the only person I was hurting with all of this anger was me. When I stepped back and put myself in his shoes I realized that he did the best he could do; not what I thought was the best, but his best. This was a monumental learning moment for me. Accepting this changed me deeply. It freed me. We've all heard it a million times, but until you experience the freedom of forgiveness, you will forever stay stuck.

Once I began to forgive I became grateful. Grateful for how the marriage ended, how quickly it ended, and for all the players who were essential to our story. Divorce gave me the best gift - the freedom to be me. My best me. My perfect me!

Truth

Each and every one of us is on a specific path. We have a mission to accomplish while we're here and we are all here for a reason.

What I have realized on my path is that the journey IS life - the memories, the good-old days - we are living them now. I have come to understand that the pain, the struggles, the challenges and sorrows have the greatest impact on our desire for change, awareness, and intent.

The most difficult times in my life were terribly sad and challenging but I am who I am because of them and I wouldn't be here without their truths. My own truth is that I wasn't truthful to myself about what I wanted and what I needed. When I finally took responsibility for that I felt relieved, and could then began to forgive myself for the years that I hid myself away. That was when I made this vow to myself:

My path will be filled with
success and failures.

I accept them all as they pave my way.

My successes fuel and accelerate my
journey. I am grateful and ready for more.

My failures teach me much about
who I am. I am thankful for them
as they teach me vital lessons.

I vow to listen to me.

The deepest part of me.

Not to be swayed by those who don't
understand or those who do not see as I do.

I vow to make me important.

I vow to be the best me.

The purest, most honest, truthful me.

I vow to be patient, understanding
and supportive of me.

I vow to strive to be all that I can be.

To work for and reach every dream.

To appreciate every step
and acknowledge that the
path IS the experience.

When a dream comes true I
vow to dream bigger.

I vow to be grateful for
everything in my life.

I vow to love me. Support
me. Empower me.

Trust

I was terrified of the future, of what my life was going to look like. Would I be able to do it alone? I wanted to know what the next step was, that what I was doing was going to work. I wanted assurance that I was going to be okay, but that's not something any of us can have. None of us knows the future. The bottom line is that we don't know what is coming next, when it's coming or how it will arrive. And what was even more terrifying to me than the unknown was the thought of staying stuck. So I had to trust.

We all have to trust. Trust that we are doing the work that needs to be done. Trust that we are exactly where we need to be. Trust that everything is going to be okay.

Trust is the one intent that has challenged me most. I strive every day to trust in my path. I try to listen to and trust the deepest part of me. I try to trust with love, strength, courage, gratitude, forgiveness and truth.

Someone once said that FEAR stands for False Evidence Appearing Real. I try to take the focus off of my fears and direct it toward trusting in my path.

Trust in your path. Trust that you are on your journey for a reason.

Patience

Patience doesn't come easily to me, it's also something I have to work on everyday. I practice patience by trying to loosen my grip on the notion that I need to control everything, surrendering to the journey and remembering that the rules and timing of the universe are not mine to define.

I have learned that time is a critical element in the healing and building process. Often we can't see or fully understanding the lessons that come from change while we are in the thick of it. It is only through reflection that the 'ah-ha's' of clarity are revealed.

The ongoing process of developing my *self* and having patience with my *self* is part of my journey. I am my best me when I inspire love, strength, courage, gratitude, forgiveness, trust and truth. And patience.

The Power of Self

Being the best, most authentic me is all I want to be. It is powerful and it is freeing. What do you want? What do you stand for? Who do you want to be? What are you waiting for?

As you embark on your journey of *self*, see yourself for all the greatness that you embody. It's time to recognize the beautiful person you are - inside and out. Your assets. Your attributes. Your strengths, gifts and talents.

Start with yourself and move forward with the intent to inspire Love, Strength, Courage, Gratitude, Forgiveness, Trust and Truth in yourself and others.

Discover your *self,* claim your future and charge ahead.

•••

Tricia Doyle Mahoney
SheEO®
PowerShe®, The Power Behind StylishShe® and
InspireShe®
www.PowerShe.com
www.StylishShe.com
www.InspireShe.com

Tricia Mahoney is the founder and SheEO of PowerShe, the parent company of StylishShe and InspireShe. PowerShe offers initiatives for women such as empowerment, networking and entrepreneurship. Ms. Mahoney built the company on the platform of helping women empower themselves via StylishShe and InspireShe.

StylishShe is the image side of PowerShe, which includes Image Consulting services and an exclusive line of women's apparel that Ms. Mahoney designed and created.

InspireShe, the inner healing side of PowerShe, is a destination for women to find inspiration, resources and products to assist them in their personal journey of discovery.

PowerShe gives women the tools and support they need to reach their goals. This transformation is reflected in increased confidence, purpose and empowerment, which ultimately impacts their relationships, attitude and approach to life.

Also by Tricia Doyle Mahoney:
StylishShe – Style for You. Your Body. Your Life.

Two

The Power of Intent
by Nora Cabrera

In the beginning there was nothing. From this nothingness came intention. From the intention came movement, from movement came expression, and from the expression came experience.

It is time to move away from right and wrong. Away from black and white, yes and no, good and bad. It is time to choose what you want to experience, and this choice must come from your individuality, not your conditioning because your individuality is YOU. You are a completely unique experience and expression of the Divine.

We are in a crisis today. So many women are thirsty to live their purpose, to live their truth, but what they continue to live is their conditioning. Conditioning is who you've been told you have to be in order to be loved, valued, respected, recognized and to feel secure. Conditioning is you, having taken on the beliefs of others as truth and reality in your own world and experience.

You cannot consciously create your life if you do not have an intention for your life. But how can you know what you intend if you do not know who you are or why you are here? If you are living someone else's version of you, you're not creating your life; you're reacting to it.

What is intent? Why does it matter and how can you put intent into practice?

According to Merriam-Webster Dictionary:

in·tent

noun \in-'tent\

: the thing that you plan to do or achieve: an aim or purpose

Intention is the spark that lights the fire of conscious action. It is also the limitless source of energy that sustains us when fear, doubt and shame try to hold us back. Are you ready take conscious action and set off on a journey to discover what you truly intend for your life? I invite you to take a little trip with me right now:

The Journey of Intention

Once upon now there exists a beautiful soul. She is magnificent and infinite in all potential, expression and radiance. She is a direct creation of the intention of the Divine: infinite love in action and expansion.

But she has forgotten. So she looks to the others. Others who are lost, who have forgotten to show her the path, to lead her, to remind her of her magnificence. She is asking the others, who are asleep, to be her guide. She believes that they hold the answers and the power for her. If she can find that perfect mentor, the one who sees her truth and beauty and potential then all will be well. So she moves from person to person asking the same questions, hoping that someone else will have the right answers to set her on her path:

Am I worthy? Do you value me?
Am I allowed to create now?
Do you love me?
Am I beautiful to you?
Do you give me permission to shine?
Is it OK if I am abundant?
Can I make the choice I really want to?

Every time she asks one of these questions she takes an unknowing step off of her path and moves further away from her truth, from her soul, from her purpose and from her authentic expression.

One day she wakes up and decides to go searching for herself on her path. As she begins her journey another beautiful soul appears on her path with a mirror in hand. This beautiful soul attempts to hand her the mirror. She doesn't want to be rude, but she has no interest in the mirror. She is on her path to serve the world and to help others, so she politely refuses the mirror.

The next day, as she steps onto the path, this beautiful soul appears again with the mirror. No thank you. She sidesteps the other beautiful soul and attempts to move forward on her path, again getting lost and asking others for permission and directions. Each night she returns to her home exhausted and still feeling lost.

This goes on for many, many days. Finally, one morning when she is again greeted by the beautiful soul with the mirror, she is tired and has less resistance and something from deep inside of her urges her to receive the gift of the mirror. She recognizes something familiar about the other beautiful being, but she is not sure what exactly it is.

She reaches out, ready to receive the mirror and the other soul gently places it in her hand. Now is her time. Knowingly, she slowly moves the mirror up to her face and curiously peers into it.

What she experiences takes her breath away. She sees the truth of herself. She experiences the truth that she is infinite love. She experiences the truth that she is infinite creativity. She experiences the truth that she is infinite abundance. She experiences the truth that she is infinite, brilliant light and knowingness. She is the unique infinite expression of the Divine in this exact point in time and space. There is nothing for her to become; she already is all that is. And she IS the intention of the Divine in motion right now.

And the other beautiful being on the path, waiting patiently for her to receive the mirror? It was her own self, waiting patiently to be seen.

So where do you begin with conscious intention on your path? I encourage you to start with these four steps:

1. Release limiting beliefs.

2. Gain clarity on what you want to create and experience in your life from your heart space.

3. Set your intentions and attach goals to them.

4. Release all attachments to outcomes and practice gratitude.

1. Release limiting beliefs:

Begin by removing the limiting beliefs and stories you've taken on in your life as 'truth' or 'reality.' The reasons you use to not live your truth right now are illusions that you need to sweep off your path. They block the truth of who you are and the truth of the limitless, infinite path you are on.

Beliefs are simply interpretations of situations, events and experiences we've had, especially when we were children trying to figure out the rules of life. But as children, we took those interpretations to heart. Many of our limiting beliefs are in our blind spot so it's important to work with someone who is experienced in helping you release those limiting beliefs. Any time you truly want something and your mind creates doubt and reasons why you can't or shouldn't, that is a limiting belief at play.

Release also means letting go of who you think you need to be or should be, in order to allow the truth of who you really are to begin to shine. We can't have the status quo while we're birthing something new. Birth is active, intense, messy, and sometimes painful. As

Brene Brown says, "You can choose courage or you can choose comfort but you cannot have both."

2. Gain clarity on what you want to create and experience in your life from your heart space:

What is it that you truly want? What experiences make your heart sing and your whole body vibrate with life and celebration? These are very important questions.

So often we think we know what we want but when we get it we discover that it didn't make us happy, or that it wasn't what we really wanted. We are constantly conditioned by outside sources as to what we should buy and how we should be in order to be happy and worthy of love and acceptance.

Fifteen years ago I was a young, impressionable go-getter. Following my dream of acting I was living in NYC, bartending while trying for my big break. In those days I spent a lot of time perusing the fashion magazines. I had to be up-to-date with the latest fashion trends if I was going to be taken seriously, right? (Hellooooo, limiting belief right here!). I remember reading about a famous actress talk about her new Cartier *Love* bracelet. For some reason, what she said about the meaning of the bracelet really resonated with me, although today I can't remember what that message was.

So I saved up my money, and when I finally had enough I walked into Cartier and purchased my *Love* bracelet. Wow! All would be well in my world now, right? When I got home and had a friend come over to help me put it on, because you can't just slip it onto your wrist, it has to be unscrewed with a special screw driver then screwed back together once its on your wrist.

The second it was secured onto my wrist I hated it! I literally felt trapped by it. I took it off and never wore it again. If you're wondering why I didn't return it to the store it's because I still use it as a reminder to be very clear about what I want and why I want it. An expensive lesson but well worth the priceless message: don't be influenced by outside forces when it comes to your deepest desires and purpose.

If you're not taking the time to get clear about what it is you truly want in your life, chances are you are being affected by outside influences: TV, magazines, music, advertisements and the internet, to name a few.

Ask yourself daily what it is you would like and why. Take a good look at your life and ask yourself, why am I choosing this? Is this what I want to experience?

3. Set your intentions and attach goals to them:

Once you're clear about what you want and what you want to experience in your life, it's time to get to work on setting your intentions and attaching specific goals to those intentions.

Remember, intention is what you're aiming for and goals are the action steps. When setting your intentions and goals avoid using the word *want*. Here's why:

Read each sentence out loud:

I want more money so I can live abundantly.

I intend to have more money so I can live abundantly.

Do you hear a difference? Do the sentences feel different to you? Please take a minute to write down the differences you felt in speaking both sentences out loud.

When I consciously use the word *want* I feel a pulling back, or a sense of not having, but when I use the word *intend* I feel a strong shot of energy moving in the direction of what I am intending.

Thinking about this prompted me to look up the origins of these words. Both *want* and *intend* are verbs, or action words. Have you ever thought about the word *want* as an action? According to the Online Etymology Dictionary, the word *want* comes from the Old Norse word *vanta,* c.1200, which means 'to lack.' Want is the active form of *lacking*. Taken back even further, from the root *eue, it means 'to leave, abandon, give out.'

Wow. Think of all the things we say we **want** in our lives. It puts things in a whole new perspective, doesn't it?

According to the Online Etymology Dictionary, the word *intend,* from Old French *entendre* c.1300, means 'direct one's attention to,' and from Latin intendere, 'turn one's attention, strain, "literally" stretch out, extend.'

Intend is powerful. By consciously intending you are actually sending the energy of creation and manifestation forward in your life. But no amount of intention will work without goals because goals move you forward onto the path of creation that your intentions have carved out for you. Your goals are the conscious action steps in the direction of your intentions; your dreams and desires. Goals are the path we set for our intentions.

4. Release all attachments to outcomes and practice gratitude:

Once you've released limiting beliefs, gained clarity on what you want to create and experience in your life from your heart space, and set your intentions and goals, it's time to LET GO!

I know. I hear the collective scream and panicked fear seeping in. "What do you mean let go?" The Buddhists call it non-attachment. Releasing expectation is very important because we often cause massive kinks in the energetic hose of manifestation energy when we try to hold on to the outcome. It usually shows up as some form of control, and control equals contraction - a lack of trust. And contraction is the opposite of expansion.

Show up for your part 100% and then surrender to the flow of energy. Step out of the way and let the Universe and Divine do what it does best. Give thanks and focus on the things in your reality that you're grateful for in your life right now in the present. There is something very potent about the energy of gratitude. When we enter into a state of authentic gratitude it feels like a portal opens up to the infinite energy that abounds from within and outside of ourselves from the Universe. There is no separation, just different possibilities and different expressions.

Conclusion: Stepping into Intention

Conscious intention is exceptionally power-ful and is crucial in consciously creating your life. Is now your time to make the choice to release limiting beliefs? Is now your time to get clear on what you truly want? Is now your time to set your intentions and goals? I believe it is or you wouldn't be reading this chapter!

Set your intention to begin now.

• • •

Nora Cabrera
Money & Business Coach, 3Blessings Success Institute
www.3BlessingsSuccess.com

For over 20 years Nora has been studying and practicing various healing modalities to help facilitate healing, growth, conscious aware-ness and authentic manifestation. She believes we are ultimately responsible for our own lives and how we create what we experience. Without awareness and knowledge, there can be no wisdom or courageous action.

Now is the time to embrace our authentic gifts and to step out into the world. As we begin to shift and facilitate healing and change within ourselves, so the world will shift and move with us. We are all interconnected and part of the whole. Our work is to love ourselves first and then to joyfully leap into the world with our gifts to live our purpose, our true destiny.

Nora is a Certified Money Breakthrough Method Coach, Certified Sacred Money Archetypes Coach, Certified Integrative Health Coach (AADP) and Certified Human Design Specialist. She has also been practicing Feng Shui for over 12 years having studied with His Holiness Grandmaster Professor Lin Yun, World Renowned Expert Katherine Metz, Nancy SantoPietro and R.D. Chin. She is the co-creator of the Vision Board Quest Coach Certification Training program with her business partner Nachhi Randhawa.

Nora believes we are creatures of habit and will re-create in our external, physical environments, bodies included, what we believe and feel inside. Her joy and expertise is to help creatives and heart-centered entrepreneurs reconnect with their authentic selves and to help them start to recreate that 'connection' in their lives so they are living beautiful, engaged, authentically successful and abundant lives.

Three

The Power of Spaces
by Wendy Sippel

Did you know that spaces, such as your home, have energy? I'm referring to the living energy of a space that manifests itself through the people who reside there, the activities they engage in and its overall spirit. All living things have energy, whether positive or negative, and every space has energy, too.

Energy is in everything: thoughts, ideas, words, emotions and actions. When there is laughter, honesty and positive communication in a space your body can feel it. Conversely, arguments and conflict disrupt energy. Positive and negative energy become embedded in everything: walls, ceilings, furnishings and drapes. Even wallpaper and paint absorb energy, and this embedded energy becomes the consciousness of the space. Think about what's embedded in your home or office. What positive or negative energy has become a part of your physical space?

Divorce, depression and death leave especially low-lying energy in a space. This negative energy drags down the space and gives rooms a heavy feeling. When parents separate and a family goes through a painful transition their house can feel like it's weighed down by a hostility hangover, and this can be especially painful for the spouse and children who remain in the residence. If you want to shake that uncomfortable feeling in your home and get everyone on track, you can try some simple energy shifters as a family. Children who are feeling anxious and angry at the inability to control changes often feel empowered by simple activities that focus on turning a page and moving forward. Taking steps to clear your space of negative energy can be an effective way to mark a fresh beginning in a familiar space.

The older or more 'stuck' the energy is, the easier it will be for us to be negatively affected by it. A healthy state of energy flowing through our living spaces is the foundation of our emotional, intellectual, spiritual and physical well-being.

As an interior redesigner and home stager I work with clients to help change the energy of their spaces. Many of my clients are realtors who hire me to change the energy in houses that just aren't selling. Although there are many reasons why a home might not sell, the two most common causes I see are families who are resisting the move and homes that are feeling the effects of negative energy, such as divorce.

A while ago I visited a 2.5 million dollar home that had been on the market for six months. The home was well loved but was also a reflection of the family's fading wealth. The couple didn't want to sell but had to. I had a conversation with them and explained that their roots were showing; they loved their home too much to release it to new buyers, and those potential buyers could feel that energy as they toured the home. The sellers and I went through the house and gently released the energy by removing family photos, clearing clutter in corners, freeing up wall space and turning on ceiling fans in rarely used rooms. This change of energy, or clearing, helped the sellers release the home and three days later they received an offer.

In a similar situation, I visited a home that had been on and off the market for a year. The only person living in the home was the male homeowner who had gone through a difficult divorce. His three children visited every other weekend but otherwise he was the only soul living there. I could feel the loneliness the moment I walked through the front doors and into the enormous foyer; the house was quiet, sad and had low-lying energy throughout its vast spaces. I could imagine a day, not so long ago, when the rooms were filled with running children, laughter and signs of life everywhere. I sat down with the homeowner and discussed some things that we could do to change the energy in the home, and then we went from room to room doing just that.

It wasn't until the end of the appointment, while talking about the changes we made, that he had his "aha" moment. He realized that he hadn't yet released the home; the home he loved, where he raised his children and loved his wife. Yes, he had prepared the house for sale by tidying up, emptying the kids' rooms and organizing his master closet, but he never said goodbye to each room, to each experience and to each memory the house held for him. He admitted to over-pricing the house because he didn't know where he was going to land. He was also letting a job transfer dictate his actions and wasn't allowing himself to feel any emotion.

The homeowner became teary-eyed at the realization that he was standing in the way of his own forward movement in life. For me, seeing him come to this understanding was like watching a light bulb turn on. We talked about his future, where he'd live and what that would look like. I explained to him that it's very difficult to release the space we're currently in unless we have a clear idea of where we're going, and that buyers can feel the hold we have over our homes. After I left I informed the selling agent that the owner was ready for a price reduction. In my experience, willingness to sell combined with a reasonable price will attract the right buyers every time.

Bringing Positive Energy into a Space

Have you ever walked into a space and had the feeling that something was off? This feeling might be the result of things such as sickness, a door being slammed too many times, loss or resentment. This negative energy could be left over from a previous occupant or created by those currently using the space. To bring positive energy into a space I have been known to wave my arms and legs and clap my hands to disturb the energy. I may look like a lunatic, but sometimes that's what it takes to shift the energy. And as important as it is to balance or clear the energy in a house you plan on selling, it's even more important to clear the energy in a space that you're living in. Harmony and positive energy should reign in all of your spaces!

There are many ways to change or rebalance energy so it feels like it's working with you, not against you. Here are a few simple suggestions to shake that uncomfortable feeling in your space and get back on track:

Walls

To create a long-lasting, energetic boost in your room purchase finely ground quartz for paint, which can be found in the paint department of home renovation stores. Hold the bag of ground quartz in your hands and send positive thoughts into it, then mix the quartz into the paint. Once the walls are painted the quartz will reflect your positive thoughts and energy and create a beautiful sheen.

Another way to infuse positive energy into a room is to write positive intentions for the space on the walls in pencil before painting or papering. In doing this you are literally creating "handwriting on the wall." Be sure to use words that pertain to the room you are painting. For instance, if you are painting your office, use words such as money, referrals, abundance and/or prosperity. If the space is intended to be nurturing use words like peaceful, tranquil, safe, secure and friendly.

Choose words that will support your intention for the room.

If your space is not ready for a makeover, write the words energetically on your walls with a capped pen so the words are written but are not visible.

Many of the early 1800's buildings had sayings on their exterior. It's too bad that we've moved away from the powerful concept of putting the handwriting on the wall. We could awaken the consciousness of the world if every home, building or structure of any kind was embedded with words of wisdom and love.

Feng Shui

Feng Shui is the ancient Chinese practice of space placement and arrangement to achieve harmony in the environment. Feng Shui, meaning *wind and water*, is not a decorating style, rather a discipline whose guidelines are compatible with many different decorating styles. A space with good Feng Shui has good flow, which is something that we not only see, but also feel.

When applying Feng Shui it is recommended that every room has something representing each of the five elements – water, wood, fire, earth and metal. It is also recommended that you incorporate colors that symbolize these five elements: black = water, green = wood, red = fire, yellow, tan and brown = earth and white = metal.

The purpose of Feng Shui is to balance the energies of a space to assure the health and good fortune of those living there. It is a powerful and inexpensive way to create positive energy in a space and, when successful, creates an environment that makes you feel centered, balanced and grounded.

De-clutter

Clutter literally sucks up the energy in a space. Negative energy needs to cling to something and it will choose the pile of magazines on the floor or the laundry that didn't make it into the hamper. You may think you're hiding your clutter, but the closet has just as much of an effect on energy flow as anything else. If there's clutter in your home, even tucked away in an attic, it's cluttering your mind as well as your body. As soon as you're finished using something, put it back where it belongs. Realize that everything you own has a hold on your attention. Clearing out clutter frees you to really make a difference in the world.

If You Don't Love It, Set It Free

Our belongings hold the thoughts and memories that we attach to them, so everything we own should lift our spirits. If something doesn't, pass it along to someone else who might enjoy it. By doing so you'll be opening up space for something more spectacular! Don't keep things just in case they might be useful someday, get rid of what you're not using and trust that your future needs will be provided for. Surround yourself with things you love, with things that inspire you and with things that lift you up.

Repair What's Broken

Feng Shui teaches us about the relationship between the parts of our house and the areas of our life. A leaky faucet or broken stove might be connected to financial challenges. Wobbly table legs or unstable chairs could be indicative of unsupportive relationships. We need to treat our belongings like precious members of our family and take care of them. Clean, mend, tighten and polish your belongings today. No temporary fixes. Give love to your belongings and you will feel a positive energy whenever you are around them.

Rearrange

Simply changing the placement of a few pieces of furniture can drastically change the energy of a space by creating new flow and rebalancing the energy. Moving furniture, even just a few inches, can make a big difference!

For effective furniture placement put yourself in the power position in that room - lay in bed, sit at your desk, relax in your favorite chair - and make sure you can see the entrance to that room. It is not good Feng Shui to have your back facing the doorway because it leaves you feeling unsettled, like you're not protected. Also, avoid having your bed directly in line with your bedroom door. Even moving your bed over one foot, so you don't look past your feet and out the door, can make a big difference in the flow of energy and your sense of peace.

Mirrors

Mirrors reflect energy and multiply what they reflect so they should be positioned in places where you want increased energy flow. Although mirrors are effective in creating balance and harmony, they can also create harm so don't place them where they will reflect anything low energy or negative such as clutter, toilets or garbage cans.

When used properly mirrors can improve energy and correct many problems, so make sure they reflect something beautiful.

Nature

Research shows that viewing nature reduces anger and anxiety and enhances feelings of pleasure. Flood your home with natural light, open up windows and doors to let in fresh air, bring in plants and hang pictures of flowers and birds or peaceful landscapes to help set a peaceful tone for each room and create calm and quiet spaces.

Cleanse with Salt

Salt has long been considered an excellent cleansing and detoxifying agent. Make a salt sachet by filling old socks with table salt and 'scrub' tables, chairs, furniture and fixtures that were at the center of arguments or suffered through negative energy. Keep the socks in the corner of troublesome rooms overnight to 'soak up' bad energy. In the morning, flush the salt down the toilet and bid farewell to bad vibes.

Sage Your Spaces

Burning sage is one of the oldest and purest methods of cleansing a person, group of people or space. White sage can be purchase loose or in ready-made bundles. Once lit, the smoke from the sage can be fanned around the location with the intent of purifying the area and removing negative energies. This is not a fumigation, just a cleansing, no need to go overboard. Concentrate on gateway areas such as windows, doors, closets and hallways. Also concentrate on the corners of the room. Use your intuition and focus on areas where the energy feels heavy.

Cleansing personal spaces of negative energy is just as important to our health as cleaning our home of germs. Looking upon your spaces and belongings with love and gratitude creates a positive, welcoming environment that supports your goals and dreams.

Live in a space that reflects the life you want to live... then live it!

•••

Wendy Sippel
The Lone Arranger
an interior redesign & staging co
817. 455.7518

Wendy Sippel, aka 'The Lone Arranger,' has been staging homes in the Dallas/Fort Worth area for the past 10 years. Her experience as a realtor in Southern California and training in redesign help sellers and their agents receive the highest and best prices for their homes.

Four

The Power of The Body

by Dr. Jennifer Beights

Your body is a powerful, beautifully created, strong and wonderful thing, capable of great feats. When you think about the miracle that is the creation of your body - the fact that the same cell that made your toenail also made your trigeminal cranial nerve, which allows sensation of the face and enables you to open your jaw to chew your food - you have to be humbled at the greatness that is within you.

Just how powerful is your body? We hear stories of a mother lifting a car off of her child who is trapped beneath and think, "Wow! Who knew an ordinary mom could be so strong? Could it be true?" Any mother faced with the mere thought of her child in danger would immediately answer with a resounding,

"Yes!" The fact is, when adrenaline surges and doubt is erased, your body is capable of tremendous strength but it often takes a crisis for your body to perform at its highest ability. Chances are you will never know the true strength of your own muscles.

Bones have great strength as well. They are designed with a hardened outer shell for tensile and direct force protection while the spongier inside resists compression, allowing them to withstand the push and pull of muscles and gravity. Although breaks in your bones can occur, bones are actually quite strong and make the perfect armor for vital internal organs.

There is much more going on within your body than just the power of muscles and bones; each and every organ also has an important function. Even the appendix, not known for its functionality, has been found useful for its ability to house probiotics, the good bugs that fend off bacterial infections.

The stomach is also quite powerful. The acids in the stomach are so strong they can dissolve the metal element zinc. You'd think that such a strong acid would eat through your tissue quickly but the stomach lining actually renews itself so quickly there isn't enough time for the acid to eat through the lining. If not for this renewing capacity your stomach wouldn't subsist, let alone readily digest foods.

Another example of the value of a particular organ is our vision coordination. Having two eyes instead of one provides depth perception, which allows us to determine when it's safe to pull out into traffic or how far to run to catch the winning football pass.

In addition to being powerful these separate organ systems must also communicate and interact fluently with each other. Take the body's extraordinary healing power for example. When you cut your finger you don't have to tell your body to produce coagulants to stop the bleeding, or tell your body to speed up the skin regeneration process to heal over that cut, because your body inherently knows how and when to act. Your nervous system sends the message from your bleeding finger up through your arm and neck and into your brain, which then sends a message back down and into your specific cells to act. Your perfectly manufactured body possesses healing potential that exceeds even the most cutting edge pharmaceutical capability. You are your own greatest healer!

This communication happens at the cellular level, which allows your body to function and is absolutely crucial to your body's intricate network. At this very second your heart is pumping blood which is carrying oxygen to the brain and getting rid of the carbon dioxide in your lungs; the salad you ate for lunch is getting broken down into nutrients and is being absorbed by the microvilli lining your small intestine, and while you are reading these words your brain is comprehending, reasoning, processing and storing pertinent fact into memory. And it's all happening in the blink of an eye - a reflex controlled by factors that your conscious mind isn't even aware of!

Is there more to us than meets the eye? Is there more to the power of your body than an intelligent meat sack carrying around vital organs?

In Chinese medicine, and in many other cultures as well, it is believed that emotional stress affects our organs, and to help our bodies with the healing process emotional clearing can be used which allows negative subconscious emotions to be released. In alternative medicine there are different emotional clearing techniques such as Emotional Freedom Technique, Neuro Emotional Technique, Emotion Code Technique and Omni Therapeutic Technique. Louise Hay does an excellent job of laying out the groundwork for the organ-emotion connection in her book, *Heal Your Body*.

Emotional clearing is a vital piece of the healing process. When someone is red from anger, they are the same shade of red as an alcoholic who has compromised his liver. Guess where the emotion of anger hangs out in the body. You betcha - in the liver. The emotion of feeling betrayal will cause the same erratic heartbeat as someone with heart disease. Guess where the emotion of feeling betrayal hangs out. Yep. The heart. It's no coincidence that what Chinese medicine has taught for over a thousand years now has the physiological research to prove it. That does not mean that anger will only reside in the liver and overjoy only in the heart, there are always exceptions to the rule. However, the generalities are as follows:

Relating to the heart:
> Overjoy, heartache, love unreceived, abandonment, betrayal

Relating to the lungs:
> Sadness, grief, discouragement, confusion, self-abuse, stubbornness

Relating to the liver:
> Anger, bitterness, revenge, hatred, depression, panic

Relating to the spleen:
> Worry, too much thinking, anxiety, lack of control, hopelessness

Relating to the kidneys:
> Fear, blaming, dread, unsupported

Relating to the sex organs:
> Shock, shame, worthlessness, overwhelmed

In order to balance the emotional system of the body and positively change your health you must clear any emotions that may cause physical stresses. The four main steps in this process are as follows:

1. Identify the emotion that is causing the stress.

2. Identify if it is a current emotion or something that you are harboring from the past.

3. Willingly want to release the emotion.

4. Peacefully re-balance your emotional center.

In my practice I use a form of Applied Kinesiology, or muscle testing, to identify the emotion that is causing a stressful state in the body. (Clearing emotions without muscle testing can be done for a general clearing but may not work as effectively).

Using muscle testing, I identify if the emotion that we are balancing is a current emotion or something from the past. This is important because as children we are unable to properly process emotions and it's surprising what silly things, no longer relevant to us as adults, will be imbedded in our cells. Traumatic events from the past are often quite apparent but less traumatic events, such as having had difficulty dealing with a new sibling or feelings of jealousy or insecurity as a kid, can also come up.

In order to clear an emotion the person must first want to release it, which can sometimes be very difficult. Forgiveness is possibly the most difficult emotion to balance out because there are some traumas that are unforgivable such as rape, child abuse or murder. If a person is unwilling or unable to forgive, that emotion can cause great damage to the body and often the traumatic experience becomes part of who you are and how you identify yourself. On an exaggerated scale people can easily become victims for the rest of their lives after being victimized by one hateful, terrible tragedy. It is important to remember that healing doesn't mean the damage never existed, it means it no longer controls our lives.

Forgiving ourselves can also be extremely difficult and inhibit someone from releasing an emotion. How many times have you beat yourself up over something from your past? Marrying the wrong person, choosing the wrong career, having unprotected sex, saying hurtful words, making an immoral decision. We are often more willing to forgive others and less willing to forgive ourselves. Maybe this is because we are unwilling to take responsibility for our actions or maybe we feel as though we deserve to be punished.

Of course, there is an exception to the "You have to want to release the emotion" rule. The exception lies with those who have a very strong emotional and physical connection within themselves. These individuals can easily release their emotional stress without much help. For example, when I first began doing emotional clearing I treated a patient named Clarissa who was from Brazil and didn't speak fluent English. Because of the language barrier I simply held her emotional points after her adjustment to give her an overall clearing without delving into the emotion work. (Because she hadn't come to me for emotional balancing, because I was fairly new at it and because there was a language gap I didn't think it necessary to do in-depth emotional clearing and just held those points based on the premise that everyone could use a little balancing). As I touched the points Clarissa started to cry and with bewildered eyes looked at me and asked, "Why am I crying?" She was one of those people who easily and quickly releases emotion without even being consciously aware of it.

The purpose of balancing emotions is to re-align your cellular frequency so it is important that you are in a calm, relaxed state when doing so. This state of peace means different things to different individuals. Some people achieve a peaceful state of mind through visualization or controlled breathing. Meditation is extremely effective in achieving a peaceful state of mind and is very efficient in ridding the body of stress. Sometimes when I meditate it is comforting for me to picture myself and The Lord as animated figures. Other times I see God dressed as a great teacher leading me in a meditation. For me, meditation and peace mean being in alignment with God but for others this may not ring true. Some people go to their 'happy place' which might be a meadow of flowers or a rainy beach, some visualize colors or numbers while others simply take long, deep breaths.

Re-balancing the emotional center can be done in many ways. I like to use the Kruger Maneuver from Omni Therapeutic Technique, as learned from Dr. Joshua Kruger. It is done by standing at the patients head, placing the index fingers over the emotional acupuncture center just above the center of the eyebrow, putting the thumbs at the crown of the head and the pinky fingers at the temples of the cranium. I feel little pulses, similar to checking a pulse at the wrist or neck, and wait for the pulses to synchronize. Emotional Freedom Technique uses tapping along the emotional acupuncture points, which has been found to be very successful. To clear emotions The Emotion Code uses magnets rolled along the spine, and Neuro Emotional Technique places the palm of the hand over the emotional center at the forehead. These are just a few of the many techniques used to clear the emotion. I encourage you to find the one that resonates and works for you.

When rebalancing the emotional center some people will instantly feel something, others won't and there is no way to determine how you will react. Some people will feel weepy, angry or sad for the next day or two; some people will feel foggy headed. Some will giggle and laugh, especially children. Some people have instantaneous emotional release, others do not. I once worked with a patient who had just returned from active combat in Afghanistan. Even with the slightest pressure of my fingertips touching his emotional center he winced in pain, so I just held my hands over his points without touching his skin. Since I was unable to feel the pulses synchronize, I had to regularly muscle test to see if the emotions had cleared.

I have seen great healing from emotional work with many of my patients. The first emotional clearing I performed was years ago on a woman named Sandra who was suffering from severe foot pain. Sandra had been to countless professionals for her pain:

orthopedists, podiatrists, massage thera-pists and acupuncturists. You name it, she tried it. Sandra stated her pain level had not changed since being chiropractically ad-justed by me on two previous visits and rated her excruciating foot pain a constant 7 on a scale of 0-10. On her third visit to my office I decided to do emotional clearing. When I muscle tested her emotions, it came up as grieving with a time period of 18 years ago.

Since this was the first patient I had ever done emotional work on I had no clue how to pres-ent the information to her, or in what manner to explain it. I remember very awkwardly stat-ing that she was holding the emotion of grief in her feet and that it was from 18 years ago. I'll never forget the look of silent shock on her face. Tears started rolling down her cheeks as she explained that 18 years ago she had giv-en birth to a baby girl and had given her up for adoption. She had kept this a secret from everyone, including her husband with whom she had three small children. He had no idea of the pain his wife had been harboring or the grief she felt for the child she never got to bond with or watch grow into a woman.

After that visit Sandra confided in her husband, set out searching for the daughter she had never met and her foot pain disappeared. Her body was able to move forward and away from the torment of emotions and her feet never bothered her again. She found her daughter and they now share a beautiful relationship.

Sometimes balancing emotions is as simple as identifying the emotion that your body is holding on to and acknowledging that it needs to balance out. Other times, however, your body needs to take the healing a step further. This is where scripture, prayer, confessions and/or affirmations come in. For example, a patient named Ginger came to me for help with multiple autoimmune disorders. Ginger's biggest complaint at the time of her first visit was nagging joint pain in her hands so bothersome that it woke her up at night. I muscle tested her and found that her body was holding the current emotion of feeling the need to control. I explained that emotional stresses can affect our physical health and that I would balance within her the current emotion of feeling the need to control. When I tried to do so nothing happened. Nothing at all. I waited for those points to balance out, but they didn't budge.

Knowing from previous conversations that Ginger was a Christian I decided to try something different. I walked Ginger through a visualization of packing up all of her stresses, especially her control issues, and putting them in organized boxes. She then pictured Jesus Christ on the cross. She had accepted Him as her savior and acknowledged that according to scripture, Jesus died on the cross not only for our sins but to carry our burdens as well. She imagined handing over her stresses and control issues to Jesus on the cross, and then imagined that those stresses were gone and acknowledged that she didn't have to carry those burdens any longer. She immediately felt light and free, her emotion points cleared and her hand pain went away. She was free from the need to control and her body was free to live life the way God intended us to live - without worry, stress, anxiety or burdens.

There are other patients who respond well to affirmations, like little Gracie. Gracie was a preschooler who was incredibly shy in public. While she was talkative and full of excitement at home, she would clam up and hide behind mom whenever she was at a restaurant, at school or anywhere around people outside of her immediate family. When we did emotional clearing on Gracie, the emotion of fear muscle tested. Just like with Ginger, after acknowledging her emotion, nothing happened. Instead of going to scripture I went to affirmations. Gracie tested with the affirmation, "It is safe for me to grow up and take responsibility for my life." I had Gracie repeat that affirmation as I held her emotional points. Things quickly cleared. A week later Gracie came bouncing into my office and her mom stated that she was a completely different child. All Gracie needed was a reminder that she was safe. It's amazing to what extent our emotions affect our life.

Sometimes affirmations and emotional balancing can affect our lives in a small way, as was the case with Stella. On her first visit Stella came to my office for overall health guidance and to address a few minor health concerns. Upon examination her minor health concerns were addressed and she was given the affirmation, "I am the power in my world and I control my own thoughts" to help balance the emotion of feeling insecure. The next week Stella was elated to announce that she had dramatically improved her tennis game. She said that she played with other women at the country club and they could clearly see that, since repeating her affirmation, her game had significantly improved. Now she is the tennis partner everyone wants for their doubles matches.

Emotional clearing is particularly beneficial for children because in today's modern world we often put great pressures on our kids without even realizing it. Sometimes just the hustle and bustle of everyday life can be overwhelming to sensitive children, as was the case with my young patient, Jessica.

Ten-year-old Jessica came to see me because she was having tummy aches. She had been to multiple doctors and had been through a multitude of tests, all of which came back normal. Upon examination it was apparent that Jessica's nervous system was affected by emotional stress. Jessica put so much pressure on herself to be the best that just waking up in the morning was overwhelming and she was unable to get through the day without her stomach bothering her. You may recall that worry and anxiety reside in the spleen meridian. In Chinese medicine, the spleen is very closely related to the digestive center and when one is imbalanced it affects the other. Thus, Jessica's stomach pain was the result of perfectionistic anxiety. I gave Jessica affirmations and homeopathics and instructed her to write her affirmations down and to tap her forehead when reciting them in her mind. This began to work for her immediately. I continue to see Jessica on a regular basis. She is still on the honor roll but she is now enjoying life and not making herself ill from the pressures to outperform everyone else.

The physical-emotional connection that allowed Jessica to overcome her stomach-aches exists in all of us. Although it is beyond physiological explanation, it is indisputable and quite powerful. So on those days when you find yourself feeling powerless to the world around you, think about the amazing things happening within your body at that very instant: your heart beating, your lungs breathing, the complex collaboration that is your body and mind. Your body is beautifully powerful. It is strong and brilliantly capable, if for nothing more than being able to function as a living being!

The average person takes over 23,000 breaths a day. Make each one encompass the power it deserves.

•••

Dr. Jennifer Beights is a graduate of Parker College of Chiropractic where she earned her Doctorate of Chiropractic, Bachelor of Science in Anatomy and a Bachelor of Science in Health and Wellness. She also earned a Bachelor of Science degree in Biology/Biochemistry from Hardin-Simmons University.

Dr. Jennifer Beights

Through her own health journey, Dr. Beights developed a passion for natural health and helping others. She believes in treating the root issues of the heart and body and takes a holistic approach, focusing on nutrition, exercise, detoxification and an overall well-being.

She resides in Fort Worth, Texas with her best friend, who also happens to be her husband. She enjoys spending time with family, cooking based on pure, whole foods, and cuddling her pugs.

*Patient names have been changed for the protection of their privacy.

Five

The Power of Image
by Lisa Avila

Styling and Image Consulting. What do they mean? Think they're only for hoity-toity people? Think again! Everyone has style. Style is unique to each and every one of us. It's what makes us different, and shows who we are to the outside world. It tells people if we are outgoing, if we are shy, if we don't like the way our body looks or if we're confident in our appearance. Our style tells our story.

I'm a stylist and image consultant. I wear what I like - the good, the bad and the ugly! I wear what makes me feel good because when I love what I'm wearing I feel great and I shine like a star in the sky. Watch out or you'll be blinded by my light!

I remember working with one of my first clients on what was probably my third Closet Outfit Creation session and I was nervous, still feeling very green in my new career. The client and I were in her closet going through her items. She had some great pieces that we used in unexpected ways with interesting jewelry and belts and other fun accessories to create some great looks. The client was happy and things were going very smoothly. We were laughing and having a great time. And then we got to the jeans.

Ok, anyone out there who says that jeans are easy to try on, wear and feel like a million bucks in is lying! They are so hard. You're rarely the same size from brand to brand. Then there is the whole fit debate: boot cut, straight leg, low rise, super low rise, skinny. The list of adjectives describing different jean cuts is mind blowing. It can throw the average woman into a tailspin that could take days to recover from.

Anyway, this beautiful woman with an amazingly curvy physique, and, might I add, curves in all the right places (but she had no idea) wanted me to help her style a pair of jeans she had recently purchased. She had succumbed to the pressures of society, which is something we all do with fashion and style, and bought something that she was uncomfortable with - skinny jeans. "They are really popular. Everyone is wearing them. My friend told me to get them, so I did," she explained. She put the jeans on and the vibe in the room instantly fell. Her shoulders slumped and her smile, along with her light jovial personality, disappeared. I could tell that she did NOT feel good in those skinny jeans. I pulled some tops from her closet and put together a totally cute outfit that fit her lifestyle and worked beautifully with the jeans. She looked adorable but she didn't feel adorable. No matter what I said, she went deeper into a hole. I realized that she was crying and my heart broke. This beautiful, smart woman was crying because a pair of skinny jeans didn't feel good on her! Notice I said they didn't feel good on her because the truth of the matter is they looked really good.

I told her to take the jeans off and put them in the trash pile. She looked at me like I was crazy but I told her that those jeans didn't deserve a place in her closet, her beautiful closet full of beautiful clothes that made her smile and feel good! And feeling good is the point of all of this and it's what I want for all of my clients. Clothes aren't meant to just make you look good; they're supposed to make you feel good, too. I want my clients to feel great, stand taller, smile wider and have that extra pep in their step. Getting rid of the skinny jeans was what my client needed to get back to feeling good about herself.

Another client who I recently worked with was feeling like she didn't have that *va-va-voom* left in her sexy engine. We all feel that way at some point; maybe after having kids or hitting that dreaded age (pick a number, any number). Often times we let society dictate how we should feel, behave and carry ourselves. We let the expectations of our grandparent's generation determine what is acceptable or unacceptable in our lives today. Well ladies, it's the 21st century. 30 is the new 20, 40 is the new 30. You get the idea - age is just a couple of digits put together to try and bring us down!

Back to my client with no va-va-voom in the engine. As it turned out, her husband saw the va-va-voom and wanted her to see and feel it too, so he contacted me. (I immediately told my husband that this was a very, very intelligent man).

I met up with my client and we went through her closet. She had nice items but they were all very practical. Now practical is great, but not when you're trying to fill up the sexy engine. The disconnect was that the client was under the impression that sexy was 'sex and trashy' all balled up into some tight, short, low cut, leave-absolutely-nothing-to-the-imagination ensemble. She said that her husband's definition of sexy was, "Tight, short, low cut and hoochie."

"Has he said those words to you?" I asked.
"No, I just know," she replied.

I explained that sexy is an attitude. She was an attractive, educated woman with a loving husband who wanted her to feel what he saw. It was very powerful.

I told her to sit back and let me work some magic. We made a plan to meet up again in a week's time after I did some shopping for her, but when I left her house I was so inspired that I immediately hit the stores and we met the next day. I had about 10 dresses for her to try on. She was shocked because they weren't short, tight or low cut. They were all very respectable, age appropriate and gasp...sexy! How dare I put those three adjectives in a sentence together! Well I just did and it felt good.

The dresses slipped right on. She stood taller and could have lit up the night's sky with her beaming smile. She finally felt what her husband saw. She got her sexy back and the rest is history.

These are just two of the many clients I have had the pleasure of styling. I've worked with clients of all ages, shapes and sizes in varying stages of life and family. Some have worked in a professional capacity for years; others are re-joining the working world after staying at home with young children. Some women are still at home with young children, working harder than they ever thought and want clothes that don't have stains or drawstring waists, that look good and feel good, too.

Whether I'm helping a professional woman revamp her style or helping a mommy re-enter the working world or just helping a cli-ent get rid of those yoga pants (absolutely nothing wrong with a good yoga pant paired with a super cute fitted jacket of course!) my goal i*s* to make every client realize that we, as women, can do ANYTHING we put our minds to!

I love what I do, and the best part of my job is working with The *She's* - my wonderful, beauti-ful clients. They are amazing, though I must tell you; I'm not a hugger. I mean, I hug, don't get me wrong. I'm just not one of those girls who greets people by hugging, unless I've known them for a while and feel close to them. I feel very strongly for my close friends and I will pro-tect them with all that I am, I just don't wear my heart on my sleeve. And even though I feel very close to my *She's,* I'm still not huggy. But sometimes a *She* leans in and what's a girl to do but hug back? Let me explain...

I had a gorgeous client who needed help getting out of a wardrobe rut. She has an amazingly successful career and is a superstar at her job, but because of her long hours she hadn't given anything back to herself. This is where I came in. The minute we met I felt an amazing connection to her because she was upfront with her body issues, the styles she liked, what she wanted to look like moving forward and how she wanted to present herself. Wow! This lady knows what she wants and that I love!

We decided to meet up to do some shopping. As we walked around the store I pulled all kinds of things. Sometimes she gave me that, "Are you are crazy?" look. I didn't care. That's my job; to nudge clients out of their comfort zones just enough to see what this big ol' world has to offer in clothing. She was game for it all and I was on cloud nine.

Now, you have to realize that when a client is with me, we're going to get to know each other very well. And very quickly. I'm in the dressing room with them, seeing them at their most vulnerable, but in a completely judgment-free zone. So she and I were off to the races. She was excited but I could tell that she was also nervous. Who wouldn't be? She was trying new styles and silhouettes, colors and textures. It was amazing!

Well, wouldn't you know, the first item that she had been leery about was a huge hit and she actually had to get it in a size smaller than what she had originally thought. Now if that doesn't put a smile on a woman's face, I don't know what does! She had the reaction that I was expecting - happiness all around. We continued on and the more she tried on, the more she wanted. I went back into the store to grab items that she had refused during our first run through. In the end we had to pare down her purchase pile and make a list of what she would buy at a later date.

As we finished our time together she leaned in and gave me the biggest, warmest, most sincere hug I've ever received from someone I've only known for a few hours. I could actually feel the gratitude; happiness and love pass from her to me in that embrace. I melted! Next to my children and husband, that's what I live for!

Working as a stylist and image consultant has given me the beautiful opportunity to help many women feel incredible about themselves and show them something in the mirror they hadn't seen before. Helping women find their personal style is powerful. It can brighten up a dark day, bring a smile to our faces, bring confidence to our being and put that extra pep in our step. But when we're feeling powerless it shows in our outward image because our outside appearance projects how we feel about ourselves on the inside. It's a sad but true fact that we, as women, are our own worst critics. I'm not saying anything you haven't heard a million times before, but we have to keep hearing it in order to change our perception.

Of course we're going to have days when we don't feel so good on the inside and that's ok, but sometimes we need to suck it up and project outwardly that we feel amazing by wearing clothes that make us comfortable but that also make us feel good, pretty, sexy and confident. You'd be amazed at how quickly you start to feel better on the inside.

Although I have confidence in my own style, I didn't know I had it in me, this styling/image consulting thing. But as I talked that sweet girl off of the skinny jean ledge, when I helped bring sexy back to the mother of two and when I helped the successful business woman out of her rut, I felt power being shared from a *She* to me. I realize that it is so much more than helping women put outfits together; I'm there to help women off of their ledges, whatever they may be. And in the process of helping each client off of their ledge, THEY have helped ME off of mine.

•••

Lisa Avila
Image Consultant
StylishShe®
www.StylishShe.com

Lisa has a passion for fashion and keeping up with the latest trends. Lisa worked in the marketing/public relations field for 15 years and has always loved to look and feel her best. Now Lisa brings her flair and creative vision to StylishShe as a personal stylist. With her keen eye and fresh approach, Lisa is able to recreate her client's look and create a wardrobe that reflects their personality and lifestyle. No matter what level of styling you need, Lisa has the enthusiasm and fashion sense to make you look great and feel great too!

Six

The Power of Patterns

by Brizel Granados

You are unique. You have been handcrafted from the finest of materials. Your existence is a miracle and your everyday is like a fine orchestra. Every moment, every interaction and every thought plays an important note that betters you and brings you to your purpose.

You are an eternal being and you are here to learn. There are no mistakes, just the necessary events that will guide you to the betterment of your soul. Everything happens for a reason and everything has a purpose. Even the fact that you are reading this book!

Consider that the only person guaranteed to always be with you is YOU. When you pass this world, just as you won't be taking your belongings, you won't be taking anyone with you.

Discovering your own truth is a matter of looking deeply into yourself and being aware and present. It isn't always easy. Everyday people mask their true selves - a defense mechanism that allows us to continue on as if everything were under control. Most of the time we don't even realize we're doing it. We don't say, "I don't know myself and I am clueless to who you are, but let's pretend that you know me and I will pretend that I know you." But by masking our true selves we are, in fact, jeopardizing our relationships.

Until we learn to be alone and learn about our true selves we will continue dealing with loneliness. Until we learn selflessness we will continue struggling with selfish attitudes, and until we unravel our anger we will continue hurting people and driving them away. Not until we claim our dignity will we stop attracting people who abuse us.

Since I was very young I have been fascinated by human behavior. This fascination led me to study Psychology in my home country of Guatemala. By a twist of fate, I came to live in the United States. Two years ago changes started occurring in my life that I had not foreseen or wanted. In an effort to soothe the pain I embarked on the most fascinating journey of my life - the search for my true self. On this journey I've learned many important things, such as the power of thought and the importance of feelings. I've also learned about the correlation between body and spirit. Basically, all that happens outside originates inside.

My curiosity and desire to heal led me to gain an even deeper understanding of myself. What started as a few questions has progressed into a complete discovery of my soul through numerology, acceptance and gratitude. In the following chapter I'll be sharing with you what I have learned along the way and what has profoundly helped me on this journey.

Numerology

Numerology is the belief that everything in the universe vibrates on its own frequency and each frequency has qualities and energies associated with it. It dates back over 10,000 years to ancient Egypt. There are three types of numerology recognized worldwide, all based upon alphabets: the Kabalistic based in Hebrew, the Pitagoric based in Greek and the Tantric based in Sanskrit. No matter which method you use, all roads lead to Rome. In other words, each method will bring the same results: YOU at your core.

Numerology subscribes to the belief that based on our birth date, we all are born with a set of numbers with properties that can vibrate in an either positive or negative type of energy and that represent a set of personality traits, tendencies and descriptions. I like to think of them as personal bar codes.

These bar codes gives us a closer look at the way we present ourselves to the outside world and the way others might perceive us. They also allow us to discover our talents - special virtues that were granted to each of us at the moment of our birth. We also learn about lessons that we carry from our ancestors and the mission that we are here to accomplish.

The first number in the bar code represents your soul; who you really are inside. The second number represents your personality; how you project yourself to others. The third number represents your Gift from God, or your talent(s). The fourth number represents previous learning opportunities that you carry with you and the fifth number represents your specific life mission.

Of course, the traits displayed on a numerology analysis can be complex, as we are complex creatures. They take on a very personal tint as one gets immersed in their significance and impact on our life story. It is truly fascinating to understand why our lives have been unfolding the way they have and it becomes easier to see the lesson in each experience.

Numerology can even trace cycle patterns back to childhood and reveal lessons intended for us at that time. Nothing happens by chance. Everything has a purpose and a reason: the type of upbringing we had, our friends, the places where we were born, simple interactions. The good, the bad and the ugly. Everything.

Surprisingly, the numbers describe us just as we are. Like a road map, they give us a clearer vision of which tendencies to avoid and which to enhance. Once these very personal traits are brought to a conscious level we then have an opportunity to change negative traits into positive ones, or at least become aware of what they are, providing us with the opportunity for improvement. As we get to know ourselves better, growth becomes easier and the work that we do within us starts emerging and touching every aspect of our lives.

Generally speaking, numerology exposes us to our deepest self, giving us a truer understanding of who we are. Consider this: "If I don't know me, how can I know you? If I don't know what I feel and who I really am, how can I know how you feel or have an idea of who you truly are?"

By seriously understanding who we are, without condemnation or judgment of any kind, we gain a deeper acceptance of ourselves. We also become more compassionate and understanding of others, which leads us to a more honest approach to life and more authentic love.

Acceptance

Only when we find a deeper knowledge of who we are can we start accepting ourselves and start being more patient with our mistakes. Only in the humility of this acceptance will we find assertiveness and self-esteem. When we condemn, we build self-defense blocks that jeopardize our work dramatically! The goal is to stop judging, stop condemning and start loving ourselves so we have something to give.

It is vital to remember that if we were perfect we wouldn't need the human experience. No one is perfect. We are all here to learn; to learn alone, to learn together and to find enough love in ourselves so we can give love to others. To share our radiance and our beauty. But we can't give what we don't have. So how can we love ourselves if we haven't really understood who we truly are? How can we give something when we haven't fully accepted ourselves? Acceptance leads to love. Acceptance and understanding replace judgment and condemnation, leaving room for a more compassionate disposition. From the premise of Karma, which in Sanskrit means to come back (every action begets a reaction) I find it crucial to learn more about attitudes that lead to love.

When we begin accepting who we are we begin to acknowledge our complete existence.

Gratitude

Being grateful is guaranteed to change our perception. When we shift our attention from grievance to gratitude, magic unfolds.

In *The Power* by Rhonda Byrne, the author explains that when we focus on the negative forces in life such as boredom, isolation, victimhood, disappointment, criticism, anger, guilt, despair and jealousy, negativity reproduces itself, feeding precisely what we need to avoid. Similarly, when we focus on the positive, good feelings begin to emerge and magnetize a more positive force, bringing us happiness. When we are happy, more of those good feelings unfold, giving us automatically more of what we want. Suddenly we become more enthusiastic, more satisfied and even more excited. Positivism attracts joy. The problems may still be there but our perception of their grandiosity will change as we feed love and joy.

Sadly though, we often fail to recognize our own creations. Sometimes we even run away from them! When we choose to look deeply our life experiences start to appear like lessons to be learned. There is no bad fate, just the necessary people and circumstances to help us grow. When we no longer perceive ourselves as mere human beings, but eternal souls capable of being transformed, our perspective changes.

There are many paths that lead to deeper introspection; some are born from curiosity, some from a particular event. Pain is what brought me here. Have you ever thought of your pain an opportunity to learn? Or, an opportunity to remember who you are? If you are struggling, would you start to feel better if you saw pain as an opportunity for growth? Problems, pain, sorrows, disappointments and anxieties are excellent guides and tools when we try to make sense of them. Problems can actually be small gifts. It only takes the decision to embark on a journey of self-discovery, to observe and be vigilant. The journey can be enlightening but it takes courage, determination and awareness.

As you begin to work on yourself, thoughts and feelings come first, doing comes last. It is vital to start being in touch with your feelings because they guide you toward what is really going on inside yourself. Be vigilant not to suppress or confuse your feelings: anger with sadness, sadness with guilt, and guilt with anger. Fear with anger and sadness. Once your feelings are identified it is crucial to promote the positive ones such as joy, gratitude, hope, forgiveness, beauty, appreciation and acceptance. Good feelings magnetize a positive force promoting better choices, delivering better actions and attitudes, which in turn, improve our lives. Positive feelings and thoughts take shape, as they become actions. And actions come back to us like boomerangs!

Deciding to live under a positive force is a deliberate choice. Your happiness is your responsibility. Ask yourself, "Am I responsible for my thoughts? Do I see the correlation between my thoughts and my actions?" You are the one who has the ability to respond, therefore create, your reality. You possess the most magnificent and fundamental gift: free will.

When you choose to see the patterns in your life, validate your intuition and look closely, big things begin to happen. Gifts are revealed and talents emerge.

Look deeply. Search inside. Get in touch with your soul.

You'll find the answers.

•••

Brizel Granados
Master Numerologist
InspireShe®
www.InspireShe.com

Brizel has been on a path of self-discovery since she was a young child. In her quest to untangle the mysteries of the subconscious mind she earned a bachelor's degree in psychology, but had many unanswered questions about healing and the mind.

Her journey of knowledge and self-enlightenment took Brizel first to Costa Rica where she studied psychogenealogy, the belief that children have emotional and psychological DNA chains in addition to physical DNA chains that are passed down from generation to generation. From there Brizel traveled to Guatemala where she became a Reiki therapist. Reiki is a Japanese technique for stress reduction and relaxation that also promotes healing. Years later, in Guatemala, Brizel discovered one of her greatest passions, Numerology.

Throughout her life Brizel has experienced great joys as well as personal tragedy, and continually moves toward enlightenment and a deeper understanding of the relationship between the physical world and the subconscious. Her goal is to share with others what she has been taught and to continue to learn and grow on this journey of life.

Brizel lives in Texas with her three boys where she enjoys Reiki and is a Master Numerologist for InspireShe.

Seven

The Power of Balance
by Stacey Stier

I used to think the balance in my life was a measure of where I spent my time. My schedule was as carefully orchestrated as the New York Philharmonic, and I was proud of that! During the workweek I would sleep eight hours, work eight hours and spend four hours with my kids, shuffling them to their various activities. On the weekend I would reserve one day for playtime and one day for housework and, when things were really balanced, I'd get in two one-week vacations a year. I had all my bases covered and got everything done. I believed in the women's movement mantra, "Women Can Have It All," and I was going to be one of those women. One problem: I wasn't happy. I didn't feel fulfilled and I didn't feel I was making a difference in the world. I was comfortable but not joyful. If one part of my day didn't go as planned, such as a sick child or a traffic jam, my stress level would soar.

Even when my carefully laid out plans and systematic schedule ran smoothly, I didn't feel balanced. I began to realize that *where* I spend my time had little to do with living a balanced life. Instead, it's about how I'm *feeling* when I'm doing what I'm doing.

This realization didn't happen overnight and certainly isn't something I've perfected. Every day I consciously ask myself, "Who am I being? How am I feeling? What am I saying to myself about the events of my day?" I now seek to *be* in a state of balance rather than measuring balance with a pie chart of my time.

There were two major life changes that prompted this shift. First, I got divorced after thirteen years of marriage and two children. About a year later I was let go from a job I'd held for thirteen years. At that time I didn't see those events as opportunities for personal growth, they just felt like failures. I didn't want to be divorced and I didn't want to be unemployed. How could I possibly manage the financial and emotional responsibility of raising my two children without the day-to-day help of their dad and without a job? It felt as if my life was falling apart.

This was when I began working on myself. I knew that if I was going to powerfully survive all of this change I had better get to work, and the work needed to start with me because I was the common denominator in these failures. I needed to feel better and, in order to feel better, I needed to clear out the emotional baggage that had me completely emotionally off balance.

I read books that inspired me and went to empowerment workshops. I got a consulting gig. I started to get very honest about how I'd gotten to this place in my life and the truth was, I hadn't even liked my job. I worked hard, I liked the paycheck and the friends I'd made there, but I didn't wake up every day with a passion for my work. The other truth was that I had been closed off and immature in my marriage. I was 19 years old when I got married, and I had my daughter at 20 and my son at 24. I had absolutely no idea what I was doing. My time and energy were spent making money and raising the children, and rarely spent working on my relationship with their dad. But, then I started to see the light, the healing process began.

Improving the sense of balance in our lives can be done is so many ways - more than I could possibly list. I'm not an expert and I'm not perfect, but I am a woman with real life experiences doing the best I can each and every day.

Here are a few things that have been especially helpful to me on my journey toward better balance in my own life:

Yoga

Bikram Yoga was a life changer for me. I took my first class in 2000 and I was pretty bad. I was tight and tense and fidgety. I was uncomfortable with the fact that I was supposed to look at myself in a mirror for 90 minutes. It seemed as if the other students performed the poses beautifully and I couldn't even touch my toes. On the drive home from that first class my mind started chattering again about the worries and fears in my life and I realized, while I had been struggling in yoga class, my only problem was how to get into the postures and survive for 90 minutes in the torturous heat. "Shut the front door! I may have just found something really valuable here. I should try that again." I bought a three month unlimited package and I haven't stopped practicing Bikram Yoga since.

Meditation

In my house I have an attic that I use for storage. Some of the items in the attic are things I'll use in the future such as Christmas ornaments and luggage, and some items are things from the past I haven't chosen to let go of yet. It's difficult to find the things I'm looking for because there is so much clutter to sift through. Similarly, I think of my mind as my emotional attic. My past, my fears, my anxieties, my beliefs and my values are all stored up there. When I search my mind for answers they often elude me because the more I think, the more confused I become. However, when I take time to clean out my emotional attic through yoga and meditation, I rid myself of the chattering thoughts that clutter my mind and then the solution comes to me like a ray of sunlight shining on the one thing in my attic I'm trying to find.

The answers are within us. Our souls know, we just need to clear the clutter in order to hear the soft voice, to see the ray of sunlight of our soul's yearning. When we connect with that part of ourselves a sense of comfort covers us like a warm blanket of truth and knowingness.

"Meditation is not a way of making your mind quiet. It is a way of entering into the quiet that is already there - buried under the 50,000 thoughts the average person thinks every day." -Deepak Chopra

Forgiveness
Mark Twain said, "Forgiveness is the fragrance the violet sheds upon the heel that crushed it."

Forgiveness is powerful. It is one of the most healing acts a person can choose. Over the years I've met many people who hang on to so much anger they see the world through an "anger lens." You probably know someone like this. Perhaps the angry person is you. This person believes that by being angry, often bitterly angry, they are somehow getting justice for the wrongdoing of their offender. Meanwhile the offender has moved on with their life and is probably spending very little time, if any, thinking about their "victim."

Buddha has been credited for saying, "Holding on to anger is like swallowing poison and expecting the other person to die." When you choose not to forgive, you are the one who suffers the most. Forgiveness is for *you.*

Oprah Winfrey defines forgiveness this way, "Forgiveness is giving up the hope that the past could have been any different."

In 1988, when I was 23 years old, my dad passed away. He was 49 years old and his body finally gave in to the effects of long-term alcohol abuse. My dad was my hero. He was a fighter pilot in the United States Air Force and retired in 1983 as a Lieutenant Colonel. I had a beautiful connection with my dad. When I was a little girl I always wanted to be with him. At the end of the day my dad would change out of his flight suit and boots into his civilian clothes and I would race to put his flight boots on and run around the house. At night we would lie on lawn chairs and stare up at the stars. At bedtime he tucked me in and scratched my back until I fell asleep. On weekends my dad played football with me and had my brother and I race each other in the backyard. He took such pleasure in my athletic ability and loved that I enjoyed sports and competition. I worshipped the ground he walked on. And then he died.

My dad died from something that I believed I could have, should have, helped him overcome. I felt so much pain and guilt because I hadn't saved him. If only I'd been brave enough to tell him how scared I was about his drinking. If only I'd been bold enough to insist he get some help, maybe he'd still be here.

It took me years to forgive myself, to give up hope that the past could have been any different. I miss my dad every day. Every year I buy a Christmas ornament for my dad and cry as I hang it on the tree because I miss him. But I no longer cry out of guilt. My dad was human and so am I. We both did the best we could from our levels of conscious-ness at the time. Forgiving myself gave me a powerful sense of freedom and peace.

Forgive others, and yourself, of past transgres-sions so you can let in the joy, peace and freedom you are meant to experience.

Gratitude

"If the only prayer you said in your whole life was 'Thank You,' that would suffice." -Eckhart Tolle

I once heard Oprah Winfrey say that the first words she thinks each morning are 'Thank you.' She said this causes her to be in the spirit of gratitude from the first moments of her day. Inspired by this I've incorporated the same practice into my own life. Of course there are still days that I get caught up in the hamster wheel of doing and accomplishing and I begin to take life for granted and complain that I'm tired or frustrated or in need of a vacation. Then, someone will walk in to my yoga studio and share their story with me. Some have had a life-threatening disease or suffer from chronic pain. Some are going through divorce, lost loved ones or are caring for elderly parents. They tell me that coming to yoga helps them powerfully deal with their current life circumstances. Hearing these stories makes me appreciate the amazing students who inspire me everyday and makes me grateful to be able to provide a space for others to heal.

My first yoga teacher used to open her bills and say thank you for each one she received. She used to say that the fact the she has an electric bill, for example, meant that she was able to enjoy all of the luxuries the electricity provided her that month: heat for the yoga room, lights in the studio, power to run her computer. Can you imagine giving thanks for your bills? Try it, you just might enjoy paying your bills, or at least have a more positive experience each month.

Being in the spirit of gratitude grounds us and centers us. Say thank you every day, even if all you can muster is being thankful that you're still breathing. It's a start.

Kindness

"Every act is an act of self definition." -Neale Donald Walsch

What would your day be like if everyone you came across in a 24-hour period was kind to you? Imagine how you would feel if no one cut you off on the highway, if your restaurant server smiled and complimented your hair-style, if your kids thanked you for making their lunch, if your husband left a sticky note on your steering wheel that said he loved you. Think about how great you would feel. So why not be that person yourself? Gandhi said, "Be the change you want to see in the world." It all starts with you.

In the movie *Toy Story*, Mr. Potato Head's wife packs his bags for a long trip the toys are going on. Since they will no doubt be up against some pretty extreme adversity, she tells him that she'll be packing his "angry eyes." I thought that was one of the funniest lines in the movie because it holds true in real life. So many people wear their "angry eyes" but kindness is a lot easier when you wear your "happy eyes" and leave the angry ones at home.

There are many ways for us to practice kindness in our daily lives. Before I say something I might regret I ask myself, "Is what I am about to say or do a representation of the greatest version of myself I aspire to be?" I always know what to do to from there. Also, don't take other people's behavior personally. Maybe your kindness will be the very thing someone needs to turn their attitude around, but even if your kindness isn't returned, you will still leave the interaction feeling good about yourself.

"My religion is simple. My religion is kindness." -Dalai Lama

Even in difficult situations when we need to deliver a tough message, we can do so with kindness. Although the truth may hurt, *we* don't have to be hurtful. As a business owner I've had to terminate the employment of several people. I've learned to take a few minutes to have an inner dialogue with myself before sitting down with that person for the difficult conversation. I deliver the message of their termination clearly, with the conscious intent of leaving them with their dignity. Whatever the reason may be for their termination they deserve to be treated fairly and with kindness. On one such occasion I had to terminate a yoga instructor whom I had given many chances. She was often late and sometimes didn't show up at all. I liked this person very much and it was heartbreaking for me because the solution seemed so simple - show up and be on time. But she didn't consistently do that and I needed to let her go because she was negatively impacting my business. I treated her with kindness, never raised my voice or tried to make her feel like a bad person, and simply told her the truth. She apologized, agreed that she needed to improve in that area, hugged me and thanked me as she left. We still see each other from time to time and there is no animosity or awkwardness between us because our relationship is clear and clean.

People are inherently good, although sometimes good people make bad choices. Not everyone will be a perfect fit in your life, but everyone deserves your kindness.

Trusting Yourself

"Life begins at the end of our comfort zone."
-Neale Donald Walsh

In 2001 I decided I was going to become a Bikram Yoga instructor. My goal was to eventually open my own studio and share this transformational practice with as many people as I could. I had made the decision that yoga would not just be a part of my life; it would also be the means by which I supported my family. Although many people in my life were incredibly supportive and excited for me, some expressed concern that I may not be able to make a living as a yoga instructor. They thought it might be more realistic for me to teach yoga as a part-time gig while maintaining a corporate position. Opinions notwithstanding, I knew it was something that I had to do.

A dear friend, for whom I admire the positive way in which she flows with life, introduced me to the teachings of Esther Hicks. Esther Hicks is an inspirational speaker and bestselling author who often uses the phrase "tuned in, turned on, and tapped in" to describe the feeling we have when we're flowing with the stream of our truest and highest expression of ourselves. This is exactly how I felt when I practiced Bikram Yoga and when I dreamed about my future as a studio owner: tuned in, turned on, and tapped in.

There were, however, some very real barriers I needed to overcome to make my dream a reality. I was a single mom with a then 16-year-old daughter and 12-year-old son, I had bills to pay and was considering attending a training course that would require me to be away for 9 weeks. Although I trusted that this was my true path, I was racked with anxiety over leaving my children for that length of time. Was I being selfish? Would my kids resent me for this decision? My gut was telling me that I

HAD to do this but I wasn't sure my kids would understand.

Because I wanted this so very badly I overcame these obstacles, one by one, and in April of 2001 set off from Dallas-Ft. Worth to Los Angeles for the Bikram Yoga teacher-training program. After the first day of driving I stopped to spend the night in a hotel. I unzipped my suitcase and found a card from my daughter. She wrote that she was inspired by the fact that I was following my dreams and doing something I believed in and was so passionate about. She told me that I was a great role model for her and, although she would miss me over the next 9 weeks, she was incredibly happy for me and proud of me. Those emotional words were a gift I'll never forget. Knowing that my daughter trusted me and believed in me allowed me to continue on my journey knowing that my kids were okay.

Choose to follow your heart as I have. Get "tuned in" to the flow by listening to yourself and being aware of how you're feeling. Don't waste your time and energy trying to change other people. Use your efforts for your own personal growth. Your strength comes from within *you*. When you learn to trust yourself, to take back the reins of your life, you'll find you are less likely to be controlled by circumstances and other people.

Today I am incredibly grateful for the support, wisdom, kindness, patience and acceptance I've received from my family, dear friends and many mentors throughout my life. It is because of these relationships I am able to see myself more clearly; the good, the bad and the sometimes ugly. I feel more balanced in my life and at the same time understand that balance is not a destination, it's a journey. I realize that each time my life starts to lean into an uncomfortable state of unbalance it's actually another opportunity for me to grow. These growth spurts can be incredibly painful, but they always birth something that is well worth the effort.

I hope these words have inspired you to consider the balance that you have, or desire to have, in your own life. That is my intention. As I said, I am no expert and I am not perfect. I'm just a woman doing the best I can from my current level of consciousness. Be kind, be grateful, be forgiving, trust yourself, practice yoga and meditation or whatever awakens your true spirit. Thank you for reading. I wish you the best on your journey.

•••

Stacey Stier
Today, Stacey owns and operates Bikram Yoga North Texas with locations in Grapevine and Arlington, Texas. She remarried in 2006 and says, "It's not perfect every day, but we challenge each other's way of thinking and being and we have a commitment to grow in our relationship. We don't hold each other responsible for the other's happiness and we'll be together as long as we both freely choose to be." Together Stacey and her husband have four children, 2 from his first marriage and 2 from hers. She and her ex-husband are friends and work together to co-parent their adult children and to let them know how deeply and purely they are loved.

Now Go.

www.ingramcontent.com/pod-product-compliance
Lightning Source LLC
Chambersburg PA
CBHW061957040426
42447CB00010B/1788